THEY HAD STORES...
WE HAD CHORES

A Town-Country Lexicon

by
Janet Letnes Martin and Suzann (Johnson) Nelson
Caragana Press
Box 396
Hastings, MN 55033

Copyright © 1995   by Janet Letnes Martin
                         and Suzann (Johnson) Nelson

ClickART and Snap Art Copyright © T/Maker Company
Quick Art ™ © Wheeler Arts

All rights reserved. No part of this book may be used or
reproduced in any manner without written permission from
the publisher. Printed in the United States of America.
Published by Caragana Press
Box 396, Hastings, Minnesota 55033

Library of Congress Catalog Card Number 94-074015
ISBN 0-9613437-7-X
First Printing

DEDICATION

THIS BOOK IS DEDICATED TO THOSE WHO KNOW:

•**How to make dolls out of hollyhocks...**

•**What a curry-comb is used for...**

•**The true meaning of these phrases...**

Shut your barn door...the cows will get out!
I can't go...my cousin is coming to visit.
Gotta go see a man about a horse.
S'pose she's got a bun in the oven?

Photo Credits:

Front Cover Photos Reproduced with Permission:

From the Collection of the **Minnesota Historical Society**
1. Street Scene from Twin Valley, MN ca. 1907

2. Vermillion Neighborly Womens Club hot lunch canning bee at school #40.

Acknowledgment:

A special thanks to clever Cathy P. across the street who came up with the title for this book.

TABLE of CONTENTS

Dear Faithful Readers of Caragana Press,

Here we are sitting at the Levee Cafe in Hastings, Minnesota. After a short spell of writer's block -- *(we've never experienced talker's block)* -- we realized all our other book introductions had been written in restaurants. We'll chat with you as we chew.

We noticed that the menu here had "Skin-on" Mashed Potatoes with Gravy. That was a new one on us, but then this town is pretty close to Minneapolis so it has to serve more than hot beef sandwiches with mashed potatoes and gravy. We noticed that they can even get watermelon in the winter here, being so close to The Cities and all that.

Well then we got talking about different kinds of food and different places which, of course, led to our views on cultural diversity. For example, for people in The City food has to look good, for people in towns it has to taste good, and for us from the country, we just want to make sure we have made enough. Similarly people in The City eat apricot marmalade, town folks buy raspberry jam, and those of us in the country make chokecherry jelly.

As good Norwegian-Lutheran mothers, we know we must transmit our cultural values and appreciation to our five lovely daughters. It is, afterall, these five girls who have provided the financial incentive for us to write and sell books about growing up in rural areas in the Midwest in the '50s.

We also just mentioned that this probably won't be our last literary effort either because after we finish paying for a combined 25 years of college for our daughters, well then of course, there will be five church weddings.........It is good we have a lot of decent material and nice memories to draw from, then.

Happy Reading no matter where you grew up; in a small town, in The City, or in the country with other normal people.

Remember Where You Came From,

Janet   *Suzann*

Chapter I

Woolworth's, Watkins &
Water Tanks

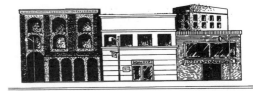

They had stores...
　　We had chores.

They went downtown to look, to browse and to be seen...
　　We went to town for parts, repairs and to bring the milk to the creamery.

They shopped...
　　We traded.

They had many kinds of shops...
  We had THE Shop.

They had many kinds of stores...
  We had grease sheds, tool sheds, wood sheds, shearing sheds, machine sheds, garages, houses, pump houses, milk houses, well houses, engine houses, brooder houses, bunk houses, out houses, barns, pole barns, loafing barns, farrowing barns, turkey barns, Quonset huts, Butler bins, potato warehouses, root cellars, storm cellars, fruit cellars, blacksmith shops, feedlots, corn cribs, granaries, chicken coops, sheep pens, lean-tos, milking parlours, summer kitchens, and trench silos.

They had barber shops...
We had Moms with bowls and wicked
clippers.

*They went to beauty salons weekly and to
beauty parlours for anniversaries and for
"boughten" cold waves...*
We went to beauty shops on prom day and
on our wedding day, but had Richard
Hudnut and rag curls the rest of the year.

They went to butcher shops and meat markets...
    We butchered our own and took it to the locker plant.

They had convenience stores...
    We had pantries.

They had bakeries...
    We baked our own.

They went to the pharmacy...
We went to the drug store.

They went to the clinic...
We went to the doctor's office.

They found variety at Woolworths...
We found variety with Watkins.

They went to the filling station...
  We went to the gas station.

They went to the post office...
  We went to the mail box.

They went to restaurants...
  We didn't.

They had water fountains...
We had water troughs.

They had train crossings...
We had cattle crossings.

They named their streets...
We named our cows.

They had elevators...
We had silos.

They had parking meters...
We had hitching posts.

They had parks...
We had woods.

They had ponds...
We had sloughs.

They had railroads...
  We had rail fences.

They had power lines...
  We had high lines.

They had water towers...
  We had water tanks.

They had ball fields...
  We had hay fields.

They measured things by blocks...
  We measured things in miles.

They had sidewalks...
  We had paths.

They had breezeways...
　　We had shanties.

They had electricity...
　　We had current.

They had City Power and Light...
　　We had The REA.

They had colored houses...
    We had white houses.

Their new houses were called ramblers...
    Our new ones were called ranch houses even
    though they looked just the same as
    ramblers.

They had sun rooms...
    We had porches.

They had attached garages...
　　We had pole sheds.

They had porch lights...
　　We had yard lights.

They had picket fences...
　　We had barbed wire.

They had privacy fences...
    We had snow fences.

They had lawns...
    We had yards.

They had bird baths...
    We had rain gauges.

They had water and sewer...
  We had cisterns and cesspools.

They had gutters in the streets...
  We had gutters in the barns.

They had basements...
  We had cellars.

They insulated their houses...
　　We banked them with straw bales, tar
　　paper or snow.

They had awnings...
　　We had dormers.

They had carports...
　　We had pole barns.

They burned gas and oil...
    We burned coal and wood.

They had the city limits...
    We had the county line.

They were fascinated by creeks...
    We were too but we called them "cricks."

They went to lake cottages...
    We went to lake cabins.

They called them mobile homes...
    We called them trailer houses.

They had guest rooms...
    We had bunk houses.

They had entries...
    We had porches.

They had indoor plumbing...
    We had outhouses.

They went to Merchants' Bank of Commerce...
    We went to Farmers' State Bank.

They took their animals to the vet...
   We called the horse doc.

They had police...
   We had game wardens.

They had letter carriers who delivered their mail...
   We had mailmen who peddled mail.

They had asphalt and blacktop...
    We had loose gravel.

They had city streets...
    We had township roads.

Then they had highways...
    We had tarvias but called them "tarveys."

Then they got freeways...
    We called them super or federal highways.

They came to intersections...
    We came to crossroads.

They had lines on the pavement to guide them...
    We were guided by ruts.

They had pot holes...
We had mud holes.

They patched their streets...
We filled washouts.

They had road graders...
We had "patrols."

They grilled on their patios...
   We cooked, baked, canned and sweat in the
   summer kitchen.

They ended their day at the Dairy Freeze...
   We ended ours in the dairy barn.

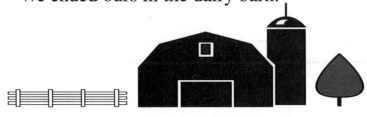

Chapter II

Dish Pans, Dust Rags & Delivering Papers

They delivered papers before school...
We did the milking.

They delivered papers...
We delivered calves.

They ran errands after school...
We did chores.

They babysat and had paper routes...
    We didn't.

They got summer jobs...
    We worked all year-round.

They got an allowance...
    We got spending money but we had to save
    some for the offering.

They used snowblowers...
    We used the grain shovel.

They mowed their lawns...
    We cut the grass.

They took drivers' training...
    We didn't have time for such and besides,
    we knew how.

They did the laundry...
   We did the wash.

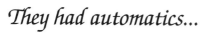

They had automatics...
   We had wringers and two tubs.

They didn't have to pull clothes out of hot water...
   We had 3' wooden tweezers to do it with.

They had "boughten" spot remover...
 We used gasoline.

They used P & G Soap...
 We used homemade lye soap.

They had Fab...
 We had Fels Naphtha.

They had Hilex bleach...
 We had Mrs. Stewart's bluing.

They had clothes dryers...
>We had clothes racks standing by the kitchen stove and down in the basement and wet clothes draped over all the chairs.

They dried their clothes indoors so they were soft and fluffy...
>We dried ours outdoors and they were stiff and hard and stood by themselves, but they sure smelled fresh.

They used clip clothespins on plastic clotheslines...

We used straight clothespins on wire lines.

They hung their panties out by the crotch so the neighbors wouldn't see what they were...

We hung our bloomers by the elastic so they would lay flatter in the drawer.

They had spray starch...

We had Niagra in a box.

They dried their frozen mittens and scarves in a dryer...
>   We put ours on top of the wood stove.

They rubbed their toes to warm them up...
>   We put our feet on the oven door.

They had steam irons...
>   We had flat irons.

They bought cleaning supplies at the hardware store...

> We bought them from the Fuller Brush Man and from ladies who sold Stanley.

They had Spic and Span...

> We had 20-Mule Team Borax.

They had Ajax...

> We had Old Dutch Cleanser.

They had Pine-Sol...

> We had Lysol.

They had "Pepto Bismal-Pink" glass wax for window cleaning...
  We used vinegar and old newspapers.

They mopped the floor with a rag mop...
  We scrubbed the floor on our hands and
  knees with a brush so we could get into the
  corners.

They took giant steps across the clean floor...
  We put down old newspapers.

They had city water...
  We had cistern water.

They had soft water...
  We had rain water
  that was really soft.

They decorated with candles...
  We candled eggs.

They had Brillo pads...
   We had chore boys.

They had dish pans and tubs...
   We had wash bowls and basins.

They had dish cloths...
   We had dish rags.

They had dust mops...
  We had oil mops.

They used a dust rag...
  We used an oil rag.

They saved old clothes for dust rags...
  We saved old clothes for grease rags.

They had wash cloths...
  We had wash rags.

They stained things...
  We varnished them.

They had flat paint...   *They had latex...*
  We had glossy.   We had enamel.

They painted their nails red...
  We painted our barns red.

Chapter III

Hearth, Hedges &
Hand Towels

They watched the dawn break...
    We watched the sun rise.

They had alarm clocks...
    We had roosters.

They had welcome mats...
    We had manure scrapers.

They watched the dusk settle in...
    We watched the sun set.

They had percale sheets...
    We had flannel sheets.

They had fitted sheets...
    We had bottom flat ones.

They had comforters...
    We had quilts.

They had pillow cases...
    We had embroidered flour sacks.

They had queen size...
    We had regular.

They had ribcord bedspreads...
    We had chenille.

They had rollaways...
    We had cots.

They had bunk beds for two kids...
    We had double beds for three kids.

They had box springs...
    We had bed springs.

They dreamed things...
    We dreamt things.

They had blond furniture...
    We had dark furniture.

They rang door bells...
    We yelled "yoo-hoo!"

They had front door keys...
    We had skeleton keys for when we went on
    big trips.

They had living rooms...
We had front rooms.

They had sofas...
We had davenports.

They had bureaus...
We had chiffoniers or dressers.

They had draperies...
We had curtains.

They had studio couches...
  We had daybeds.

They had wall-to-wall carpeting...
  We had scatter rugs.

They had Venetian blinds...
  We had pull-down roll-up shades.

They had matching arm covers...
　　We had doilies.

They had chandeliers...
　　We had flourescent tubes.

They had Early American...
　　We had Early Attic.

They had fireplaces...
    We had kerosene stoves.

They had air ducts...
    We had chimney pipes.

They had lava lamps...
    We had hurricane lamps.

They had recliners...
　　We had rockers.

They had runners...
　　We had doilies.

They had placemats...
　　We had table cloths.

They had luncheon cloths...
　　We had table cloths.

They had cedar chests...
    We had hope chests.

They had vaccum cleaners...
    We had carpet sweepers.

They had step stools...
    We had step ladders.

They had wicker baskets...
We had bushel baskets.

They had waste baskets...
We had trash cans.

They had garbage pails...
We had slop pails.

They had Eurekas...
We had rug beaters.

They had combination windows...
    We had storms and screens.

They had ash trays sitting out...
    We hid them under houseplants.

They had floor-standing ashtrays...
    We had pipe stands.

Their houses had attics...
    Ours had storerooms.

They had bar stools...
    We had milking stools.

They had booster chairs...
    We had normal chairs with Monkey Wards
    and pillows on them and tied the kids in
    with dish towels.

They had kitchen cabinets...
    We had kitchen cupboards.

52

They had linen and damask table cloths...
    We had oil cloths.

They had Mix-Masters...
    We had egg beaters.

They had oven mitts...
    We had pot holders.

They had pots and pans...
    We had kettles.

They had Dutch ovens...
We had roasters.

They had electric fry pans...
We had cast iron skillets.

They used pressure cookers...
We used the hot water bath method.

They had refrigerators...
    We had ice boxes.

They had freezers...
    We had deep freezes.

They had cobbler smocks...
    We had full-sized aprons that made sense.

They had canister sets...
    We had Karo Syrup pails.

They had countertop canister sets for flour and sugar...
    We had built-in, pull-out wooden bins.

They had faucets...
    We had pumps.

They called them hand towels...
    We called them "good-for-nothing" sizes.

They used aluminum foil...
We used tin foil.

They used cellophane wrap...
We used waxed paper.

They bought their wrap...
We used liners from cereal boxes.

They had breakfast nooks...
We had kitchen tables.

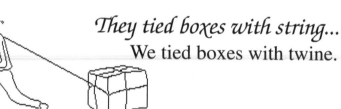

They tied boxes with string...
We tied boxes with twine.

They drank from shiny, colored tin glasses...
We drank from jelly jars.

They had stainless steel and porcelain sinks...
We had wash pans and dish tubs.

They had silver-plated flatware by Rogers...
We had stainless steel knives and forks.

After they had been married 25 years, they got sterling silver...
After we had been married 25 years, we got silver-plated tableware with Betty Crocker coupons.

They had silver service sets...
We had onion sets.

They had Lennox...
We had Boonton.

They had spinet pianos...
We had upright pianos.

They put icicles on their Christmas trees...
We called it tinsel.

They had baby strollers...
> We had baby buggies with manual brakes
> and the kids sat straight up.

They had baby cribs...
> We had corn cribs.

They had play pens...
> We had pig pens.

They had landscaping...
We had lilacs.

They had lilac hedges...
We had lilac bushes.

They had privet hedges...
We had wind breaks.

They had privacy hedges...
    We had shelter belts.

They had shrubs...
    We had Caragana hedges.*

They had flowering crab trees in the front yard...
    We had crab apple trees in the orchard.

*(See Cream Peas on Toast for definition of Caragana)

They planted roses...
    We planted "glads."

They grew mums and carnations...
    We grew zinnias and bachelor buttons.

They picked peonies and pansies...
    We picked rocks and mustard.

They had blue spruce...
We had Norway Pine.

They had fly swatters...
We had sticky fly paper.

They had electric fans...
We opened windows.

They had new things...
We had used things.

They bought new things...
We bought Brand New things.

Chapter IV

Fresh, Frozen &
Fried Foods

They charged groceries...
We traded for staples.

They had "boughten" food...
We had homemade.

They had a snack...
We had lunch.

They had brunch...
We had breakfast and then lunch.

They had lunch...
We had dinner and then lunch.

They had dinner...
We had supper and then lunch.

They had homogenized and pasteurized...
We had raw and separated.

They had two-percent or skim...
We had whole.

Their milk came in a carton or a bottle...
Our milk went from a cow to a pitcher.

They used half-and-half...
　　We had real cream.

They bought Dream Whip Whipped Topping Mix in a box...
　　We whipped our own.

They bought sour cream...
　　We used sour milk.

They bought ice cream...
   We made ice cream.

They had face cream...
   We had fresh cream.

They had creamy peanut butter...
   We had chunky.
   (If we were going to pay good money for it,
    it better have some bulk.)

They had cream cheese...
 We had cottage cheese.

They had Cheese Whiz...
 We had Velveeta.

They ate ham and cheese...
 We ate pickled pigs' feet and headcheese.

They had oleomargarine...
 We had butter.

They had butter mints...
  We had buttermilk.

They had running water...
  We had well water.

They had preserved and frozen...
  We had canned and fresh.

They had Grade A eggs...
    We had pullet eggs.

They had eggs over easy...
    We had eggs fried in bacon grease.

They had Melba toast...
    We had rusks.

They had instant freeze-dried coffee...
    We had egg coffee.

They drank Postum...
    We drank Ovaltine.

They ate Malt O' Meal...
    We ate Cream O' Wheat.

They had hot cereal...
   We had oatmeal.

They had flapjacks...
   We had pan-a-cakes.

They had thin bacon...
   We had thick salt pork.

They mashed their food...
    We mushed it.

They bought peaches by the pound and ate them...
    We bought them by the lug, lugged them home and canned them before they went bad.

They picked apples for apple pie...
    We used "ground-fall."

They had crescent rolls...
    We had crescent wrenches.

They had waxed fruit for centerpieces...
    We used the salt and pepper shakers.

They had trivets...
    We had crocheted hot pad covers.

They drank hot chocolate...
    We drank cocoa.

They had Kool-aid...
    We had lemonade.

They bought Mogen David...
    Our non-Norwegian Lutheran neighbors
    made dandelion wine.

They drank Orange Crush...
   We drank Nesbitt's.

They drank pop...
   We drank Watkins nectar.

Then, they drank soda...
   So we drank pop.

They had sugar cubes...
We had sugar lumps.

They stirred them...
We dunked them.

They ate sweets and confections...
We ate candy and pulled taffy.

They had barb-e-cues...
   We had picnics.

They ate Sloppy Joes...
   We ate barb-e-ques.

They ate hot dogs...
   We ate weiners.

They ate sweet corn...
   We ate field corn...if we had to!

They had facial peels...
We had banana peels.

They had potato peels...
We had potato peelings.

They bought Crisco...
We rendered lard.

They made casseroles...
　　We made hotdishes.

They made cake from a box...
　　We made cake from scratch.

They put icing on it...
　　We put frosting on it.

They had pastries...
   We had lard doughnuts.

They bought Aunt Sally's cookies, Hydrox cookies and Animal Crackers...
   We baked ginger snaps, hard molasses ones
   and raisin rocks.

They used store vanilla...
   We bought it from Watkins.

They had jam...
    We had jelly.

They ate apricot marmalade...
    We ate chokecherry jelly.

They used paraffin...
    We used wax.

They had corned beef...
    We had dried beef.

They had escalloped corn...
    We had scallopped corn.

They used ground round...
    We used hamburger.

They had goulash...
  We had hash.

They had honey-baked ham...
  We had clove ham.

They had speghetti...
  We had macaroni hotdish with cornflakes
  on top.

They had pot roast...
>   We had roast beef and gravy on spuds and
>   white bread.

They ate sardines...
>   We ate kippers.

They had walleye...
>   We had perch or sunnies.

They had lima beans...
  We had baked beans.

They had balogna...
  We had baloney.

They had thuringer and venison sausage...
  We had summer sausage and deer sausage.

They had Spanish olives...
    We had pickled pigs' feet.

They had taco sauce...
    We had ketchup.

They had tortillas...
    We had lefse.

They had appetizers...
    We worked up an appetite.

They ate cukes...
    We ate pickles.

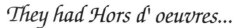

They had Hors d' oeuvres...
    We had relish trays with beet pickles, dill
    pickles, corn relish, 7-day pickles, bread
    and butter pickles, watermelon pickles, etc.

They had Log Cabin and Aunt Jemima syrups...
    We had Karo or brown sugar with water.

They used soy sauce...
    We used soy beans.

They had giblet stuffing...
    We had bread dressing.

They had Dairy Queens...
    We had Dixie Cups.

They had pizza pie...
    We had rhubarb pie.

They had strawberry shortcake...
    We had angel food with whipped cream and
    strawberries.

They got Candy Livesaver Books for Christmas...

We got Cracker Jack.

They had <u>Betty Crocker's Cookbook</u>...
We had <u>Let's Cook with Gail</u>.

They had Cream of Broccoli soup...
We had Cream Peas on Toast.*

* See Cream Peas on Toast: Comfort Food for
  Norwegian-Lutheran Farm Kids (and Others)
  by Caragana Press.

Chapter V

Heat Lamps, Horehound Drops & Hickeys

They had Band-aids...
    We had bandages.

They bought Band-aids...
    We ripped sheets.

They had vaccinations...
    We had shots.

They went to the clinic...
We doctored.

They were treated by Dr. Ostergaard...
We doctored with Ostergaard.

They had heating pads...
We had heat lamps and hot water bottles.

They got sun-burned and then tanned...
We blistered and peeled.

They had thermometers...
We had hands on foreheads.

They perspired...
We sweat.

They sweat...
We were wringing wet.

They got zits...
    We got pimples.

They got pimples...
    We got boils.

They got acne...
    We had bad complexions.

They got blisters...
We got callouses.

They got bunions...
We got corns.

They got fever blisters...
We got cold sores.

They got liver spots...
  We got skin cancer.

They had real strokes...
  We had sunstrokes.

They got hickeys...
  We got the hiccups.

They got false teeth...
   We got uppers and lowers or choppers.

They had glasses...
   We had specs.

They got dizzy...
   We got spells.

They bought cough drops...
  We bought horehound drops.

They bought Throat Discs...
  We mixed honey with lemon.

They got massages...
  We got rub-downs.

They had Vasoline ointment...
We had carbo-salve.

They had Johnson's Baby Powder...
We had corn starch.

They used Visine...
We used boric acid.

They had Vicks VapoRub...
   We had mentholatum.

They wrapped a sock around their neck...
   We made a poultice.

They had iodine...
   We had mecurochrome.

They had steamers...
   We had croup tents over whistling kettles.

They had Pepto-Bismal...
    We had milk toast and Brach's pink mints.

They had Milk of Magnesia...
    We made prune sauce.

They treated themselves with hot milk and toast...
    We ate mustard soup.

They had toilet paper...
    We had peach papers.

They got pregnant...
We were P G or
in a family way.

They started to show...
We seemed to be putting on weight.

They had maternity clothes...
We didn't.

They went into labor...
   We were always laboring.

They had labor pains...
   We "took ill."

They went to the delivery room...
   We had mid-wives.

They worried about appendicitis and tonsilitis...

    We worried about arthritis and mastitis.

They were concerned about psoriasis and neurosis...

    We were concerned about coccidiousis and trichinosis.

They worried about gaining weight...

    We worried about cows bloating.

They worried about measles, mumps and diptheria...
>   We worried about rabies, anthrax, and hoof-and-mouth disease.

They were concerned about oak wilt...
>   We were concerned about wheat rust.

They were terrified of polio and tuberculosis...
>   We were terrified of polio and tuberculosis.

They got the measles...
    We got the chicken pox.

They got the mumps...
    We got ringworm.

They pulled slivers out with a tweezers and alcohol...
    We used a hot needle followed by Watkins Petro-Carbo Salve.

They had hysterectomies...
    We had female troubles.

They had their baby teeth pulled by a dentist...
    We had ours pulled with a string and a door knob.

They went to the dentist for a toothache...
    We got out the cloves.

They had smelling salts...
    We had "Snap outta it."

They had half-wits...
    We had dim-wits.

Eventually they went to the State Hospital...
    We ended up at the funny farm.

They wore copper bracelets to fight rheumatism...

We used Watkins Menthol Camphor Ointment.

They bought Deep Heeting Rub...

We had Watkins Red Liniment (with a Trial Mark on the bottle) and witch hazel.

They became exhausted...

We got dog-tired.

When they passed away, they went to mortuaries...

When we were goners, we went to funeral parlours.

They had coffins...
We had caskets.

They had cemeteries...
We had graveyards.

Chapter VI

Floor Shifts, Flash Lights & Foot Feeds

They drove around in cars...
    We motored.

They had automatics...
    We had sticks.

Their cars had accelerators or
gas pedals...
    Ours had foot feeds.

They parked in garages...
  We parked in sheds.

They had driveways...
  We had two tire tracks.

They had Cadillacs...
    We had cattle racks.

*Their second vehicles were wood-paneled
station wagons...*
    Ours were pick-ups.

They had a second car for The Wife...
    We had an uninsured one for the field.

They had campers...
  We had toppers.

They slowed down for kids in the street...
  We slowed down for cows on the road.

They had head-bolt heaters...
  We brought the batteries into the house.

They reved their engines...
    We kicked the tires.

They slipped the clutch...
    We knew better.

They kept an eye out for traffic cops...
    We looked for the highway patrol.

They filled her up (at the filling station)...
　　We put on gas (at the gas barrel).

They filled her up with premium...
　　We called it ethyl.

They bought cans of oil at Mobil's flying red horse...
　　We bought barrels at the Farm Co-op Store.

Their cars had glove compartments...
   Ours had cubby holes.

They kept maps and flashlights in theirs...
   We kept toothpicks, shotgun shells, *snus*
   and twine in ours.

*They had St. Christopher statues on their
dashboards...*
   We had NESW balls on ours.

They had flashlights...
  We had trouble lights.

They had mud flaps...
  We hung canvas strips on the back of the
  pickup.

*They bought "Swept-wing" Dodges with big
tail fins in 1957...*
  We bought this same car six years later.

They didn't buy Kaisers, Hudsons, DeSotos, Frazers, Studebakers, Nash Ramblers, Metropolitans, Packards or Henry J's more than once...

We didn't either--except for parts.

A few of them bought Edsels...

We just said, "*Ja*, that's sure something, then."

They kept stadium blankets in the back of their cars...

> We kept extra gas cans in the back of the pickup.

They protected their new seats with bath towels...

> We protected ourselves from springs poking through pickup seats by sitting on old Army-green boat seat life preservers that had seen their better days.

They kept a comb and mirror on the visor...
  We kept elevator records, a carpenter's
  pencil and a can of *snus* there.

*They had wobbly-headed dogs in the back
window...*
  We had foam dice in the front window.

They used their ashtrays...
  We used the wide open spaces.

They pulled boats with their cars...
    We pulled hayracks with our pickups.

They used studs...
    We used chains.

They had four on the floor...
    We had three on a tree.

They had power steering...
    We had steering knobs.

They had customized cars...
    We left them as they were when we got
    them off the used car lot.

They bought two-tones...
    BIG DEAL!

*In '55 some of them even bought three-
tones...*
    BIG HAIRY DEAL!!

They had Hollywood mufflers and straight pipes...

We had plain mufflers until they fell off and then they sounded like Hollywoods.

They had fender skirts...

What earthly good are they, then?

Some of their cars had four headlights...

We had side spotlights for poaching.

They had whitewalls...
　　We had plain tires.

They had spinners...
　　We had hubcaps.

They had tubeless tires...
　　We had inner tubes.

They went for joyrides in convertibles...
　　We stood on the running board going out to
　　the field.

They drove their cars to the A & W Drive-in...

    We kept spouted water jugs in the pickup.

When their cars broke down, they took a cab...

    When ours broke down, we stayed home.

Their cars had dual antennas...

    Ours didn't even have radios.

They dragged main street...
    We dragged summer-fallow.

They had grass seed spreaders...
    We had manure spreaders.

They had 22" lawn mowers...
    We had 8' sickle mowers.

They had hoes...
    We had plows.

They bought stock market shares...
    We bought plow shares.

They had geranium planters sitting outside...
    We had corn planters.

They had bike racks...
  We had cow stanchions.

They had garden claws and trowels...
  We had disks and cultivators.

They used old tin cans for seedlings...
  We put old cans on top of the tractor exhaust
  pipe to keep out moisture.

They gave oncoming cars a full-hand wave...
We just raised our index finger from the steering wheel.

Chapter VII

*Tabbies, Toads &
Thistles*

They had Red Owl...
We had barn owls.

They had canaries...
We had crows.

They had parakeets...
We had barn swallows.

They fed their animals "boughten" pet food...
  We fed ours tablescraps.

They had Easter bunnies...
  We had jack rabbits.

They had goldfish in a bowl...
  We had suckers in the stock tank.

They had Guinea pigs...
　　We had Guinea hens and real pigs.

They had kennels...
　　We had pens.

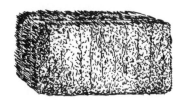

They had straw...
　　We had bedding.

Their pets had water dishes...
Ours drank our of one pound Harvest
Queen Coffee cans.

They had spiders...
We had Daddy-long-legs.

They had spider webs...
We had cob webs.

They brushed their animals...
We curry-combed them.

They rode with a saddle...
We rode bareback.

They had tabbies...
We had mousers.

They knew how many cats they had...
    We didn't know from one day to the next.

They caught frogs...
    We caught toads.

They called them skunks...
    We called them polecats.

They had cockers and terriers...
    We had shepherds and collies.

They kept their dogs on a leash...
    Ours had free rein.

They gave their dogs baths...
    Ours bathed themselves in "cricks" even if
    they had tangled with a skunk.

They had hunting dogs...
  We had cattle dogs.

They had inside dogs...
  We had outside dogs.

Their dogs slept in doghouses...
  Ours slept in the barn.

They showed dogs at dog shows...
We showed them at 4-H and at the county fair.

They had pedigrees and purebreds...
We had half-breeds, mongrels, mutts and Heinz 57 varieties.

They cashed in pop bottles...
We sold gopher tails.

They clipped their pet poodle's nails...
    We trimmed our cows' hooves.

They trimmed their dog's hair...
    We sheared sheep.

They had their pets neutered...
    We castrated pigs.

They had a garden in the back yard...
　　We had a field in the back 40.

They had Canadian whiskey...
　　We had Canadian thistle.

They counted tomatoes per plant...
　　We counted bushels per acre.

They watered their lawns...
We prayed for rain.

They thought Alfalfa and Buckwheat were Little Rascals...
We knew exactly what they were!

Chapter VIII

Tee-Shirts, Training Bras & Trousers

They wore long white stockings...
  We wore long brown stockings.

They kept theirs up with a new garter belt...
  We kept ours up with a used garter belt
  strengthened with safety pins.

They wore "seamless"...
  We wore seams.

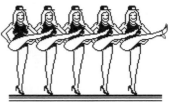

They changed into play clothes...
We changed into ever-day clothes.

They grew out of their clothes...
We wore them out.

They got new clothes...
We got hand-me-downs.

They had "boughten" clothes...
 We usually had homemade clothes.

They ordered through Sears Roebuck and Speigels...
 We ordered from Montgomery Wards and
 Aldens.

They had long johns...
 We had union suits.

They wore short underwear...
 We wore long underwear.

They wore undies...
 We wore snuggies.

They wore panties...
 We wore bloomers (dull Pepto-Bismal pink).

They wore tee shirts...
    We wore strap shirts.

They wore training bras...
    We wore undershirts and baggy tops.

They wore sweater bras...
    We wore jumpers.

They wore slips...
     We wore petticoats.

They wore crinolines...
     We wore can-cans--
     "Alice Long fifty-yarders!"

They wore half slips...
     We wore full slips.

They wore girdles...
> We did too, but we saved our "good girdle"
> for Sundays and for "dress up."

They had merry widows and long-lines...
> We had corsets.

They had nylons and hosiery...
> We had cotton stockings but called them
> silk.

They wore sox...
We wore socks.

They wore Bobbi sox...
We wore anklets.

They bought quilted slippers...
We had homemade ones Grandma knit.

They got mukluks...
We made slippers out of new wash cloths
and crocheted a border around them.

They had baby doll and shorty pj's...
We had long flannel mended hand-me-down
night gowns.

They wore scuffs...
We went barefoot.

They wore shorts...
We wore pedal pushers.

They had middy blouses...
We called them sailor tops.

They wore dusters...
　　We wore robes.

They had bathrobes...
　　We wore outside clothes to the outhouse.

They had housecoats...
　　We had housedresses.

They had cabinet Singers...
　　We had Old Home treadles.

They had pinking shears...
We had all-purpose scissors.

Their clothes were made from material...
Ours were made from dry goods.

They bought their material at a fabric store...
We bought our dry goods at the Mercantile.

They had raglan sleeves...
We made set-in sleeves with gussets.

Their clothes had snaps...
Ours had hooks and eyes.

They had buttons...
We had buckles.

They had zippers...
We had buttons.

Their tops had darts...
Ours had bust-lines.

They wore belts...
We wore suspenders.

They had sweater guards...
We had sweater clips.

They wore shoulder pads...
We had muscles.

They had dress clothes...
    We had church clothes.

They had casual clothes...
    We had ever-day ones.

They wore vests...
    We wore weskets.

They wore "biblesses"...
We had bibs.

They had coveralls...
We had overalls.

They had khakis...
We had jeans.

They wore chambray...
We wore denim.

They had dress pants...
    We had church pants.

They had pleated pants...
    We had baggy pants.

They had slacks...
    We had trousers.

They wore bow ties...
    We wore real ties and sometimes string ties.

They had car coats...
　　We had storm coats.

They had shorty coats...
　　We had jackets.

They wore stadium jackets...
　　We wore long jackets.

They had pea coats...
　　We had sailor jackets.

They had herringbone coats...
  We had tweed coats.

They had camel coats...
  We had dark-colored ones that wouldn't
  show the dirt.

They had shrugs...
  We had sweaters.

They had raincoats...
> We had rain scarves.

They had rubbers...
> We had overshoes (four-bucklers for ever-
> day and zippered for church).

They had Kickerinos...
> We had winter boots.

They had ear muffs...
    We had ear flaps.

They had mufflers...
    We had long scarves.

They had gloves...
    We had mittens.

Then they had mittens...
    So we got choppers.

They had tennis shoes...
　　We had canvas shoes.

They had pumps...
　　We had high heels.

They had cordovan penny loafers...
　　We had dark slip-ons.

They had saddle shoes...
　　We had black or brown Oxfords.

They had felt poodle skirts...
　　We had gathered circle skirts (with a side
　　zipper).

They had skirts with knife pleats...
　　We had skirts with box pleats.

They had full skirts...
　　We had flarey skirts.

They had swim caps...
　　We had bathing caps.

They had swim suits...
　　We had bathing suits.

They had swim trunks...
　　We had bathing trunks.

They wore scarves...
    We wore kerchiefs.

They had red bandanas...
    We had red hankies.

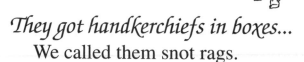

They got handkerchiefs in boxes...
    We called them snot rags.

Chapter IX

Pigtails, Purses &
Pop Beads

They wore caps...
   We wore hats--
     straw or cowboy.

They carried wallets...
   We carried billfolds.

They wore sunglasses or shades...
   We had brims or squinted.

Their men wore rings...
    Ours didn't.

They wore wrist watches...
    Our men carried pocket watches.

They wore tie tacks...
    Our men wore tie clasps.

Their men itched from centennial beards...
   Ours did from barley beards.

They wore Mennen Skin Bracer...
   Our men had Old Spice.

They used electric shavers...
   We used straight-edged razors.

They carried handbags...
    We had purses.

They used Kleenix...
    We used hankies.

They had mirrors...
    We had looking glasses.

They had tote bags...
    We had shopping bags.

They had umbrellas...
    We had rain bonnets.

They had beauty marks...
    We had moles.

They wore brooches...
    We wore pins.

They wore pearls...
    We wore pop beads.

They had pierced ears...
    We wore clip-on earrings.

They plucked their eyebrows...
    We plucked chickens.

They had rubies, emeralds and sapphires...
    We had Mothers' rings.

They had compacts...
    We had loose powder.

They wore rouge...
    We pinched our cheeks for color.

They used eyebrow pencils...
    We used eyedrops.

They had Avon's To a Wild Rose...
    We had Evening in Paris.

They had pony tails...
    We had pigtails.

They would weave their hair...
    We would braid ours.

They put their hair in French rolls and doughnuts...
    We put ours in twists and buns.

They used Bobby pins...
    We used hair pins.

Then they used spoolies and clips...
    So we used Bobby pins.

They wore hair barrettes...
    We wore hair clasps.

They used curling irons...
  We used curling rods.

They used Du Sharme...
  We used wave set.

They slept with a bouffant, poofy thing over their curls...
  We slept with a dish towel tied over ours.

They took morning showers...
    We took Saturday night baths.

They had bath tubs...
    We had galvanized wash tubs.

They had Breck...
    We made egg shampoo.

They had Tame Conditioning Rinse...
    We used vinegar.

They had AquaNet hair spray...
    We had hair nets. (Beaded, for fancy doings).

They had tooth powder...
    We had baking soda.

They had Colgate with Gardol...
    We had tooth creme.

They had Cashmere Bouquet...
    We had Jergen's.

They had Ivory and Lux...
  We used Palmolive and Lava.

They had hand cream...
  We had hand lotion.

They used cotton swabs for cleaning ears...
  We used thin, worn-out wash rags.

They got shoe shines...
   We gave ours spit shines.

They had Shinola...
   We had brown shoe polish.

They had hair cream...
   We had hair oil.

They had emery boards...
    We had nail files.

They had manicure sets...
    We had nail brushes with curled handles.

They had Ban and Arrid...
    We had creams, powders, 5-Day Deodorant
    pads and dress shields.

They had dresser sets...
   We had an unmatched brush and comb.

They had talcum powder...
   We had talc.

They looked for crows-feet...
   We looked for the crow bar.

They had "Moddess Because"... *
   We had rags.
                (*Remember: Moddess Rhymes with "Oh, Yes.")

When visiting The City, they used the Ladies' Room...

When visiting The City, we used the toilet.

On a date, they went to the Powder Room...
On a date, we went to the can.

At home, they went to the biffy...
At home, we went to the outhouse.
(Eventually, we all went to pot!)

Chapter X

Sports, Shorts & Sewing Cards

They had parties...
We had get-togethers.

They entertained...
We served.

They went sailing...
We went baling.

They went sledding...
We went sliding.

They played a hi-fi...
   We played a phonograph.

They listened to '45s...
   We had '78s.

They had transistor radios...
   We had vacuum tubes.

They had television...
    We had a radio.

They had TV trays...
    We had a picnic table.

They watched Ed Sullivan...
    We went to our aunts in town to watch
    Lawrence Welk on Saturday night.

They watched Queen for a Day...
We listened to Ma Perkins.

They took home movies...
We had box cameras.

They took pictures...
We took snaps.

They had flash cubes...
We had flash bulbs.

They went to the movies...
　　We went to show.

Their favorite actress was June Allison...
　　Ours was Ma Kettle.

Their favorite actor was Erroll Flynn...
　　Ours was Pa Kettle.

They watched movie stars...
    We watched shooting stars.

They wanted to be ballerinas...
    We wanted to be ballet dancers.

They played with face cards...
    We played Rook cards.

They chewed Chiclets...
    We had Sen-Sen.

They could waltz...
    We did the two-step.

They did the tango...
    We did the hokey-pokey.

They did the butterfly...
    We did the polka.

They did the fox trot...
    We did the schottische.

They did the jitterbug...
　　We did the bunny hop.

They danced to Whoopee John...
　　We got whooping cough.

They went on vacations...
　　We took trips.

They went to the Black Hills...
　　We went to the State Fair.

They took a suitcase...
We took a grip.

They stayed at the Sunset View...
We stayed with relatives.

They sent postcards...
We sent penny postcards.

They had desk phones...
We had wall phones.

They called the operator...
We got through to central.

They had private lines...
We had party lines.

Their number was 2409...
Ours was two shorts and one long.

They got the daily...
    We took the newspaper.

They subscribed to the Fargo Forum...
    We got *Decorah Posten*.

They read the comics...
    We read the funnies.

They went on Daylight Savings Time...
    We called it fast time.

They had rowboats...
    We had stoneboats.

They preferred boating...
    We preferred fishing.

They had inboards...
    We had Johnson 5-horses.

They used night crawlers...
    We used angle worms.

They had life preservers...
    We had life jackets.

They swam...
    We bathed.

They took swimming lessons...
    We had haying.

They had Radio Flyer wagons...
     We made some out of peach crates.

They had go-carts...
     We had scooters.

They swung at the play ground...
     We "swang" from the track in the hay barn.

They had tents and tent poles...
     We had blankets over clothes lines.

Their tents were made from canvas...
　　We called it tarp.

They used skewers for hotdogs...
　　We used plain forks, whittled twigs or
　　untwisted lead coat hangers for weiners.

They smoked cigarettes...
　　We chewed snuff.

They called it Copenhagen...
　　We called it *snus*.

They went bowling...
    We played horseshoes.

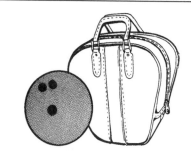

They played chess...
    We played Chinese checkers.

They played golf...
    We played croquet.

They had pocket knives...
We had jack knives.

They went after rewards...
We went for bounties.

They played summer ball...
We had summer fieldwork.

They played tennis...
  We played badminton.

They had tricycles...
  We played "Skip to my Lou."

They were in track and field...
  When we weren't in the field we had gunny
  sack races and played tug o' war.

They played bantam ball...
We raised bantam hens.

They had baseball jerseys...
We had jersey cows.

They shot baskets in the driveway...
We shot birds in the barn.

Their big brothers came home "on leave"...
Ours came home on furlough.

They collected coins...
We collected napkins.

They collected stamps...
We collected pencils.

They had Betsy-Wetsy dolls...
We made hollyhock dolls.

They had doll houses...
   We had playhouses in the woods.

They had bridge clubs...
   We had homemakers' clubs.

They had canasta clubs...
   We had birthday clubs.

They did cross-stitching...
   We crocheted.

They made jersey potholders on frames...
   We had sewing cards and yarn.

They did handiwork...
   We patched.

They knitted caps...
   We darned socks.

They had hula hoops...
   We had embroidery hoops.

They had pajama parties...
   We had sleep-overs.

They belonged to Scouts...
   We were 4-H members.

They went to Scout Camp...
   We went to 4-H Camp.

They had greased watermelon contests...
   We had greased pig contests.

They read the Ladies' Home Journal...
  We read the Farm Journal.

They read Redbook...
  We read Readers' Digest.

They read Sports Illustrated...
  We read Popular Mechanics.

They read National Geographic...
    We read The Dakota Farmer.

They read Better Homes and Gardens...
    We read Successful Farming.

They read the World Almanac...
    We read the Farmer's Almanac.

They got the Ideals holiday editions...
    We got the *Julehefte* annual editions.

They had big Fourth of July celebrations...
   So did we.

We both played: Pom Pom Pull Away, Tug O' War, King of the Hill, Keep Away, Fruit-Basket Upset, Musical Chairs, Red Rover Red Rover, Anti-I-Over, and One O'clock Two O'clock...

   We usually won!

Chapter XI

Teachers, Tablets &
Tornado Drills

Their schools had many rooms...
  Ours had one.

They had many teachers...
  We had one.

They had hot lunch...
  We had cold.

They took a bus to school...
    We walked.

They had lunch boxes...
    We had Karo Syrup buckets for lunch pails.

They had sandwiches cut on the diagonal...
    We had whole slices wrapped in wax paper.

Their sandwiches were made with "boughten" bread...

Ours had homemade bread.

They had water fountains...

We had a water pail with a dipper.

They had fuel oil furnaces...

We had coal stokers.

They had lavatories...
  We had outhouses.

Their teachers had gone to state teachers' colleges...
  Ours had gone to Normal School.

They had a "high school" superintendent...
  We had a county superintendent.

They had blackboards...
   We had slates.

They had maps on portable stands...
   We had wall-mounted maps.

They had lyceums...
   We had school programs.

They had new-styled, flip-top desks...
We had old-fashioned, flip-seat desks.

They pushed a button to ring the bell...
We pulled a rope.

They had school carnivals...
We had ice cream socials.

They had fountain pens...
    We had inkwells.

Then they got ballpoints...
    And we got fountain pens.

They had Eversharps...
    We had No. 2 pencils from the local
    insurance company.

They had rubber binders...
We had rubber bands.

They had mathemetics...
We had arithmetic.

They said the Pledge of Allegiance...
We had Opening Exercises.

They had free-style drawing...
    We colored inside the lines.

They had art classes...
    We painted-by-number at home.

They learned cursive...
    We learned the Palmer Penmanship Method.

Many of them had spiral notebooks...
We all had tablets.

The town kids that did have tablets had colored pictures of animals on the front cover...
We had Big Chief tablets.

They had shiny, store-bought bookcovers...
We made bookcovers out of brown bags.

They had Civil Defense drills...
We had tornado drills.

They had phy ed...
We had recess.

They had lockers...
We had cloak rooms.

They did calisthenics...
We did exercises.

They had gym suits and pinneys...
    We didn't.

They had gym shoes...
    We went stocking-footed.

They carried sports clothes in duffel bags...
    We carried them in brown bags.

They played basketball...
    We had basket socials.

They played softball...
    We played kittenball.

They had diving boards...
    We had rope swings.

They had swing sets...
    We had tire swings.

They played in the orchestra...
  We played in the band.

They took organ lessons...
  We took piano lessons.

They had majorettes...
  We called them baton twirlers.

They played the trumpet...
We played the cornet.

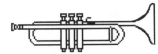

They played violins...
We played fiddles.

They practiced on real instruments...
We practiced on fluta-phones.

They had gymnastics...
  We had "acrobats."

They had see-saws...
  We had teeter-totters.

They saw movies...
  We saw film strips.

They put on plays...
  We put on skits.

They had declamation...
  We had recitations.

They had Thespians' Club...
  We had put on sketches.

They had Show-and-Tell...

They played with marbles and cat eyes...
  We played with steelies or ball bearings.

They had guests come to their classrooms...
  We had visitors.

They went on field trips...
  We went on town trips.

They had donkey basketball...
   We had the county fair.

They had winter concerts...
   We had Christmas programs.

They got off on "snow days"...
   We got off for silo-filling.

In bad weather, they went home at noon...
   We went to our designated storm homes.

They had school sidewalks...
    We had school cake walks.

They played hockey...
    We played hooky.

They chewed Beemans and Black Jack...
    We chewed wheat and wax.

They read Nancy Drew mysteries...
We read the Hardy Boys.

They read the Bobbsey Twins...
We read the <u>Five Little Peppers</u>.

They learned about Dick and Jane and Sally...
We learned about Flicka, Ricka and Dicka.

They sang "Jolly Old St. Nickolas"...
  We sang "*Jeg er så glad.*"

They played dodge ball and football...
  We played Captain May I and Leap Frog.

Their school year memories were kept in a Yearbook...
  Ours were in the Annual.

They "went with" the opposite sex...
    We "stepped out" with them.

They "dated"...
    We "kept company."

Their boys "went calling"...
    Ours went "courting and sparking."

They were "seeing" one another...
    We were "fond of" each other.

When their girls were "going steady," they tied the knot in their headscarf over their chin, wore their boyfriend's letter jacket and basically showed off...

When our girls were "going steady," it had better be with one of the same faith or they were in big trouble.

When they "went steady," they wrapped yarn around his ring...

We made it fit by wrapping it with adhesive tape.

When they went steady, they wore little plastic pink, blue or white clip clothespins called Going Steady pins...
    We wore our anklets pulled up instead of folded down.

When they went steady, they wore their collars up in back and exchanged class rings...
    So did we.

They had memory work...
   We had memorization.

They memorized things...
   We learned them by heart.

They took year-end tests...
   We took year-end examinations.

They went on to the state college...
    We went to the local ag college.

They paid for rent and food...
    We paid room and board.

*They were done with school
by Memorial Day...*
We were done by
Decoration Day.

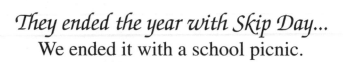

They ended the year with Skip Day...
We ended it with a school picnic.

Chapter XII

Services, Suppers &
Solos

They had Confirmation classes...
    We "read for the minister."

They were Confirmation students...
    We were confirmands.

They had Confirmation classes on Wednesday nights...
    We read for the minister on Saturday
    morning.

They had catechization...
    We had public questioning.

Their sermons were given by the minister...
    Ours were given by the pastor.

They had several ministers...
    We had one pastor.

They had year-round service schedules...
  Ours changed seasonally.

They had pipe organs...
  We had pump organs.

They had organ benches...
  We had organ stools.

Their organist got paid...
  Ours didn't.

They got the Red Hymnal...
  We hung on to the Black one.

They had a church choir...
  We all sang, harmonized
  and memorized.

They used the Revised Standard Version...
We used the King James.

When their service was over, they played the chimes...
We rang the bell.

They had education hour...
We had Sunday School.

They went on Luther League retreats...
　　We went to Bible Camp.

They had Released Time...
　　We had Religious Instruction.

They had Vacation Bible School in June...
　　We had haying.

Their women went to Circle...
    Ours went to Ladies' Aid.

They sold their stuff at rummage sales...
    We gave it away at clothing drives.

They supported those in the mission fields...
    We supported the foreign missions.

They had soup suppers during Lent...
    We had Harvest Festivals in November.

They had Easter breakfasts at church...
    We had Mission Suppers.

*Their mothers got orchid corsages on
Mother's Day...*
    Ours wore carnations.*

    * Red if their mother was still living.
      White or pink if she wasn't.

They had PTR (Preaching, Teaching, Reaching)....
We had chalk talks given by missionaries.

They had Tent Meetings when traveling evangelists came through town...
We had altar calls with evangelists but nobody felt comfortable about it.

They parked on the street...
We parked on the church lawn.

They had to drive to the cemetery...
Our graveyard surrounded
the church.

At funerals, they had a paid male soloist who sang "How Great Thou Art"...
We had Mrs. Nels Knutsvig (leader of the Women's Triple Trio and pianist for the children's Christmas program) sing *"Den Store Hvite Flok"* for free.

They had furnace vents along the side aisles...
We had a big grate in front of the altar.

They had Christmas Day services when it fell on a weekday...
We didn't.

They sang the fancy version of "Away in the Manger"...
We sang it the right way.

They were engaged...
  We were "promised to."

They had florists for their weddings...
  We had generous neighbor ladies.

They had bridesmaids and groomsmen...
  We had two attendants "stand up" for us.

Their processional was "Trumpet Voluntary"...
Ours was "Here Comes the Bride."

They had a groom's dinner the night before the wedding...
We had a shivaree a week after the wedding.

Their bride's father walked her up the aisle...
Ours gave us away!

Their soloists sang "O Perfect Love" and got paid...

Ours sang "Entreat Me Not to Leave Thee" for a corsage.

They kissed at the altar...

We smiled.

*Their wedding receptions were served by
ladies from the mother's circle...*

Our classmates were our waitresses and they
each got a nice, frilly, see-through organza
apron with a folded lace hanky for the
pocket made by the bride herself.

*They tied cans and shoes on the back of the
newlywed's car...*

We put Limburger cheese on the manifold.

For their honeymoon, they went to Yellowstone...

If we had one, we went to Duluth.

They generally went on a honeymoon...
We generally settled right in at the homeplace.

They carried the bride over the threshhold...
We both carried water to the barn.

A new generation of chores was beginning......

ORDER FORM for <u>They Had Stores...</u>

(A Town-Country Lexicon)

Name_____

Address_____

City_____St_____Zip_____

No. of Copies_____ @ $6.95   **Subtotal**: $_____

        (Canada $8.95)

Plus Postage & handling (per book)

   1st Class $2.50 per book $_____

   Book Rate $1.50 per book $_____

(Maximum postage cost for multiple orders: $6.00)

   MN Residents add 6.5 % Sales Tax $_____

                         TOTAL: $_____

Send cash, check or money order to: Caragana Press

                                    Box 396

                                    Hastings, MN 55033

I

ORDER FORM for <u>They Glorified Mary...</u>
(A Catholic-Lutheran Lexicon)

Name_____

Address_____

City_____St_____Zip_____

No. of Copies_____ @ $6.95   **Subtotal**: $_____
      (Canada $8.95)

Plus Postage & handling (per book)

  1st Class $2.50 per book $_____

Book Rate $1.50 per book $_____

(Maximum postage cost for multiple orders: $6.00)

    MN Residents add 6.5 % Sales Tax $_____

                          TOTAL: $_____

Send cash, check or money order to: Caragana Press

                                    Box 396

                                    Hastings, MN 55033

ORDER FORM for <u>Cream Peas on Toast</u>

Name_____

Address_____

City_____St_____Zip_____

No. of Copies_____ @ $9.95   **Subtotal**: $_____

Plus Postage & handling (per book)

   1st Class $3.00 per book $_____

Book Rate $1.50 per book $_____

(Maximum postage cost for multiple orders: $6.00)

   MN Residents add 6.5 % Sales Tax $_____

                TOTAL: **$_____**

Send cash, check or money order to: Caragana Press

                                  Box 396

                                  Hastings, MN 55033